LIFE STINGS
THE OVERCOMER

TAWAN D WILLIAMS

LIFE STINGS – THE OVERCOMER

For information contact :

(Kingdom Empowered Enterprise)

http://www, Kingdomempowered.com

Book and Cover design by oliviaprodesign

ISBN: 978-0-578-40824-8

Published by: Kingdom Empowered Enterprise LLC

First Edition: November 2018

10 9 8 7 6 5 4 3 2 1

CONTENTS

SOLVE THE PUZZLE

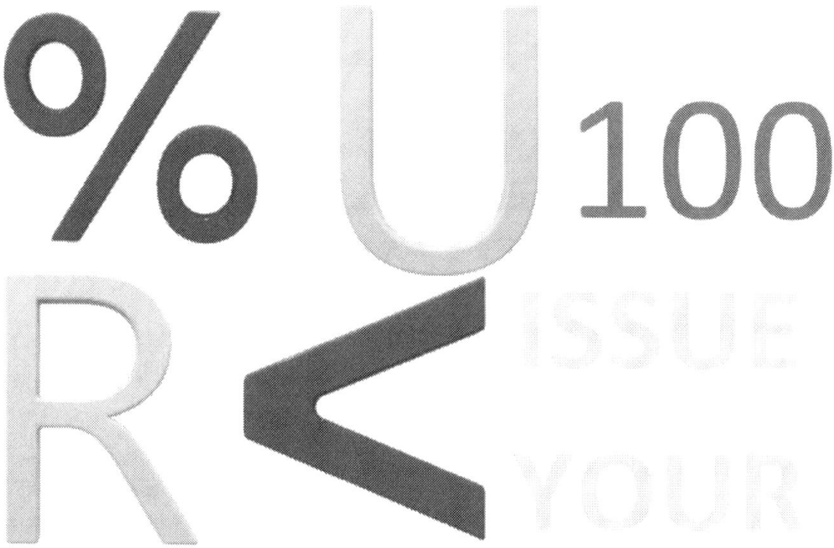

U R 100% GREATER THAN YOUR ISSUE

INTRODUCTION

"To build a forest, you must first plant and nurture the seeds."

Hi, let me start by saying congratulations and thank you for deciding to become great in this life of uncertainties, as well as pursuing your destiny which God has given to you from the foundation of time. My name is Tawan Williams formally known as Tawan-G in my young whippersnapper, Thunder cat, Firecracker, Shorty, Young buck days and now known as Pioneer T. D. Williams or Pioneer T. Will for short. I'm still young, but I've matured out of being a whippersnapper and all the other accolades.

I was born and raised in what we refer to as the hood, the great city of East Saint Louis, the city of champions. I'm writing not because I'm a writer, nor because I need money. But, I'm writing this book because I needed to share with you something that changed many lives including mine. However, most people take it to the grave with them. Not because it is a secret, nor are they hiding it. Most didn't share and coach others because it is a calling and a gift that most are fearful of. It requires time, dedication, passion and most importantly, transparency.

You must be real and straight up as you lead. No one wants to willingly re-live every traumatic, painful, dark, ugly, sickening, and despiteful experience that occurred in their life just to try to help someone they don't even know or someone that may not even care enough to listen. I know this because I have done the same severally. However, God gave me grace and mercy to live through my trauma, which also gifted me with the ability to tell my story. Prayerfully, I will be able to coach you in your journey to greatness through my pain.

Welcome to
the City of East St. Louis, IL
City of Champions

CHAPTER 1

In the Beginning

"It is not death that a man should fear, but he should fear never beginning to live." Marcus Aurelius

The lights were flashing red and blue, sirens sounding, cars begin to slow and pull to the side. He is in high hope and desire that the lights flashing isn't in pursuit of him but only needs an open lane. So, he transitioned to the far-right lane and began to slow down to allow the police to pass. "Oh no," He whispers as the lights pull directly behind him.

He begins to profusely sweat, "what am I going to do?" He whispers to himself. Not trying to let his wife and kids hear the discomfort in his voice. The last thing he needs is his wife and kids to panic and do something that will make the officers nervous.

They didn't know he had been drinking and is carrying illegal substances as well as a firearm in the vehicle. A felon with all of this in his possession will guarantee that he will be in for the big one. He contemplated running but, his kids and wife would be put in immediate danger.

So, he pulls over slowly and places the vehicle into park. He checks to make sure everyone is in their seatbelts. As he wiped the sweat off his forehead and brow. He instantly starts to coach himself on what it is he needs to say. He slowly lowers the window and nervously waits on the officer to arrive.

Once the officer arrived at the window, he brusquely uttered, "Mr. officer please allow me to explain!" The officer sharply replied, "Sir, I need your license, insurance, and registration please." "well…, sir, I do not have either a license nor insurance with me because I was rushing my wife to the hospital and left my personals at home and my registration is bombarded by my wife's legs."

Officer, "My wife is in labor and my son is ready to arrive into the world so, I'm in great pursuit of the emergency room." He explained. The officer abruptly interrupted him with a large smile and gaping eyes of joy. The officer begins to gather himself and smiles at his wife the officer then reveals that those words have brought boundless joy to my father and may have changed his life forever.

Well, congratulations! "I will escort you to the hospital." The officer shouted with great excitement. This man was ecstatic with what just happened. He praised God all the way to the emergency room. He quickly changed his music from earth wind and fire to Sherly Caesar and the Winans. He placed his cross back on his rearview mirror and began to quote scriptures. He immediately became such a man of God for he just received favor from God, big time. He was about to go down for a very long time, but his prayers were answered.

They arrived at the hospital, he brusquely parked, however, careful to not hit any nearby cars for he wasn't so eager to draw any more attention to any law enforcement officers. So, he parked and began to shout at the paramedics, "HURRY! HURRY! My wife is having our baby!"

The paramedic immediately took her in and began to deliver the baby. "Push! Push! Hun, Push! He's coming! He's coming out; oh my God, I can see his head, keep pushing!"Amazing, my purpose child is here he said to his wife.

He was born, February 1985 around 3 pm, in the great City of Champions, East Saint Louis IL. This is the day the world stopped spinning for just a moment. This is too confusing to me, because, I thought I was the purpose child. What is this my dad talking about purpose child?

"So, was I a mistake?" I mumbled under my breath, with my head slumped deeply toward the floor. My heart was broken, for I just knew that I will soon be forgotten. You mean to tell me that I'm not the last child? I now have a baby brother. Everyone seems to be so happy. Am I not still standing here? I thought I was going to be the last child, the one that will get all the attention. Now, I have a baby brother that is taking all my love and attention.

What is this? My purpose child, really? Ha-ha-ha… purpose. I'm the purpose child, me. "He was a mistake!" I uttered to myself with great disappointment and envy. As my mom and dad gazed into my baby brother's eyes and rub his hair with so much illuminating joy and compassion. It just made me sick to my stomach and no one knew how it was affecting me.

100 NEGROES SHOT, BURNED, CLUBBED TO DEATH IN E. ST. LOUIS RACE WAR

MAN-HUNTING MOBS BURN 60

CHAPTER 2

Divine Appointment

"Be aware of divine appointments in your life. They can take you places you never imagined you would go." Pam Russell

Have you ever done something, and it served a purpose much greater than you originally planned? For example, helping an elderly person with their groceries and they suddenly have a heart attack, due to your small gesture you were there to help save their life? I have learned that doing what we call a small gesture will most of the time turn out to be an opportunity for you to receive a great reward.

I truly believe that you are that small gesture from your parents because they gave birth to you. You will become that great reward to us all as long as you continue to never give up nor give in to defeat, failure, or haters that are all in your face with negativity.

I was that hater that was in my brother's way for so many years. I was so caught up in his lane that I couldn't stay on track in my own life.

Until one day my mom got so fed up after receiving my brother's grades. He had all F's maybe one D that she turned to me and went off. Blamed me for it all. She told me that I needed to be a better brother and stop bullying him. I didn't understand for a long time.

One day I was thinking back on how my older brother treated me and how it made me feel and how I felt forgotten by my family and how jealous I was of my brother. It wasn't his fault and truthfully it wasn't reality. I started to examine my ways and learned that I was hurting internally, and my brother was the outlet. My family loved me dearly and as I began to believe that, my relationship became better with them. My brother is my ace boon coon now. Yes.

I learned that in the midst of pain, you have a choice to make a difference for better or worse. What choice will you make? If you are still breathing, you can fulfill your purpose in life. It doesn't matter if you are 5 or going on 60 years of age; it is never too late to complete your purpose if your heart and mind agree. Tell those haters to kick rocks and step, as my wife says to me when I want to watch the game over her chick flicks. You can laugh, I laugh every time she says it.

We must stay on course because you have a purpose to accomplish. Steering off course, will cause an accident with another person's purpose. Try driving in the wrong lane and see how discombobulated things get between you and everyone else on that road. The same goes for your purpose; if you are not in your lane, you will cause accidents not only for yourself but for others around you as well. Get it, got it. Good, let's move on.

Now, I must warn you, this book may help to develop and equip your mindset for success. If you're not ready to become successful in your thinking, please continue to read this book and by the end of it, you should be ready. In other words, no excuses are accepted, so read the book and take notes.

At the age of two is when it all began. My first experience of pain was at my family barbeque where volleyball was the highlight of the day. My uncle jumps and spikes the ball for the winning point, as my uncle lands, he lands on me. What scared me the most was my mom's response, because she screams at the top of her lungs, "My baby! My baby! You landed on my baby." My mother's scream shook the world, as her eyes began to fill with tears and her hands began to shake. "I'm getting the car," my father said to my mother; "We need to rush him to the hospital. I think it may be broken."

Sure enough, the doctor returned with the x-rays. "Mr. and Ms. Williams, your son's foot is broken in two places." the doctor says, while he slowly points at the x-ray with a suspicious and concern look on his face. "I must ask how this occurred Mr. and Ms. Williams?" said the doctor. My parents began to try to get their story straight before speaking and I blurt out, "my uncle jumped on me," as the tears continue to pour down my cheeks into my mouth mixing a salty taste to my sweet delightful freezer pop. I didn't know any better, but my parents cleaned it up by explaining that it was an accident during a volleyball game. So, it wouldn't be considered child abuse. Close call!

My uncle felt so bad that he brought me fruit baskets and apologized to me every time he came by. I healed so fast, I knew it was because of the fruit. I still today prefer them over Zuzu's and wam-wam's. That injury changed my eating habits which in turn changed my health. What was meant to break me strengthened me. I managed to walk out of my cast in a matter of two weeks.

If you can just understand that when something or someone exposes a weakness, that is your opportunity to become stronger than you were before. I was born bowlegged and this incident brought awareness to that. However, I grew out of it and I truly believe it had a lot to do with my injury.

Message: You don't work on things that you don't know needed to be fixed. So, allow people that have your best interest at heart to be very real and candid with you. It's in your best interest even though it will hurt. That experience didn't slow me down.

Over time, I began to find other things to do like play with fire. Yes, I became a firebug, and after I set our house on fire twice, I learned that it can be very dangerous for me and my family. The first time I set the front room on fire was playing with matches. By God's grace, it was put out before it burned the entire house down. However, it caused major damage to the house.

You would think I learned that playing with fire has dangerous consequences, but I set the house on fire a second time.

The second time I set the house on fire I was doing the same thing but, late at night while everyone was asleep. This time it got extremely bad. I never meant to drop the match either time. But, it burned my fingers and I didn't know what else to do. So, I dropped it and the couch lit up so fast that I immediately ran to my parents and told them what has happened.

My dad was a nude sleeper. I learned in this situation what commando meant. Nevertheless, he got up and woke my brothers and sisters up while my mom opens the front room window for us to climb out. I guess they didn't have the key to the door at that time and all the other windows had bars on them. So, my dad began to throw us out the window into the hands of my mom.

My mom liked cactus plants and I remember my dad not being able to go out the window because he was still in commando mode.

However, he was able to get the door open. By this time, the fire reached out and touched my dad's behind. I never saw my dad move so fast with so much freedom. He didn't even try to cover himself with his hands. He was a very confident man I guess.

That was so scary, the thought of losing my family from an unwise decision. My parents had a long talk with me about what I've done but, they did it differently then I was accustomed to. They thanked me for waking them up and telling them what I did.

It is important to confess your wrongdoing immediately because it can be life altering in so many ways. It can be a matter of life or death. The longer you wait, the more damage it can cause. However, that didn't stop me from playing with fire; I just needed to find a safer way to do it.

I began to build fires in the yard until I set the yard on fire and it began to spread toward the trees and the house. Now, we didn't have a water hose to put it out so, I had to take cups of water to pour onto it, that didn't work. Only by the grace of God, it didn't catch onto the trees and house. The yard was toasted.

Well, a few weeks later; we had the best-looking grass in the neighborhood, thanks to me. Enough is enough; my mom tore my behind up. Never again did I play with fire, until I found interest in fire-breathing dragons. So, once more I had to at least try to breathe fire.

I grabbed my mom's rubbing alcohol and loaded my mouth up, lit the lighter and mission accomplished. It was a success until it reached the kitchen curtain. Well, the house didn't burn down this time, but my behind was on fire from another beat down from my mom. My mom was a wonderful mother; she was the most loving mother I knew. However, it came with a correction which I began to understand as I got older.

Pain is necessary; pain will require you to think with strong determination to make the best decision in the present moment.

I was what you would call a Dennis the Menace in the hood. I had a green big wheel that I called the green machine. Everybody in my community knew when I was coming, and they began to brace themselves because I was always up to something.

For some reason, everyone in my community began to take their belts off or began to pick a switch out of the tree when they saw me coming. That was weird; maybe you can tell me what that was all about?

Ok, I will just say it. I was bad as hell and everyone knew it. They said if I came back down their street, they were going to beat my behind all the way back to my house. Pause! While I try to stop laughing. Ok, I can continue with my story… My God, I was bad to the bone, only by the grace of God.

We desire to be butterflies far too soon. We rush the most important part of the process. The caterpillar stage of our life is the stage where growth and strength occur. We must allow that process to run its course. During this course of life, it will be challenging times, uncomforting and disappointments. However, this is the season of our life that we grow to be strong enough to break out of our cocoon and develop our wings that will take us to a sustainable successful future.

CHAPTER 3

This is my why

"Experience life in all possible ways- good-bad, bitter-sweet, dark-light, summer-winter. Experience all the dualities. Don't be afraid of experience you have, the more mature you become."

Oaha

My why are my life situations, no one who has lived a life that stings should want anyone to experience the hurt that I have felt. I had no choice but to do what I was called to do.

No man that worked so hard to succeed in life should give up now; who in their right mind would do that?

I'm hungry for change in the lives of our children and our children's children. Something must change and I'm up to that. I'm seeking to get a grand slam! Our bases are loaded! Get ready to take off! Let's Go!

Yes, my life has had some ups and downs; I learned that if you don't get up and do something, you won't get nothing. For that, doing nothing (failure) multiplied by something (Results) = Nothing (failure).

Formula for failure is: 100% x 0 =0

There was a story about a man that waited thirty-eight years for someone to help him into the water of miracles (success) because he was unable to do so himself, due to his circumstances.

One day, a very wise man came to him and asked him why he was laying there in failure and disappointment. Shortly after hearing him complain about the life he had to live and how people would never assist him in his struggle, he began to ask him: Why don't you just get up and walk to your blessings and miracles?

The wise man got so tired of his complaining that he had to basically tell him boldly to get up and walk. Finally, the man rose above his problems and began to live an extraordinary life from that point on.

Therefore, I do what I do because it is possible. Yes, it is possible. No matter what the problem or struggle is. It is possible for you to come up and out of it immediately. You must stay focused on what it is you had in your plans to accomplish. Do not become distracted by what's happening around you.

The Attack -I could have died:

Asian Giant Hornets is one of the most dangerous Hornets in the world and I was introduced to them at an early age. This is the day I will never forget, the day I almost died. It was a sunny summer day, where every kid in the community would come together prepared for a game of softball. Yes, the good old game of softball.

My teen brother and teen sisters were setting up the field and I knew this day, I will get the opportunity to show them what I've got. I was 6 years old, soon to be 7-teen if you know what I mean. I was no longer the baby and was so ready to show them what I've got.

This is the day that I will no longer be too young to play. But, my brother and sisters obviously had it in their mind that today will not be that day.

"Hey! Pick me! I'm playing." I yelled out to my older sister.

"No, you not playing! Go home Tawan," my sister yelled with the remember the last time voice.

"I'm not going nowhere." as I ran in the opposite direction of my sister.

See, I was bad but not stupid; I did want to live to see another day.

So, I began to walk with my newly found pet stick. I started to contemplate on how I can disrupt their game and figured I'll get a mirror and blind the batter as they come up to bat. "Where will I get a mirror from?" I asked my pet stick, no answer. So, I allowed that idea to expire as I slowly walked to the half-shattered concrete, half-broken wooden porch. It had a slightly sunken foundation with a surrounding molded wooden rail.

In great anger, I sat on top of the unsupportive rail and watched them play and have so much joy and fun. I began to dig into one of the many holes along the support post in the wooden rail seeking to cause destruction and enlarge the hole. Behold, out came a hornet.

I began to tell my pet stick that this hornet has no clue that it's about to meet its demise. As I slowly adjust and mentally prepare to take my anger out on it. This hornet decided to humble me, it called out its entire swarm. It had to be hundreds of them. Immediately I knew I lost that battle. I ran, screamed and cried until I noticed the sun setting and the moon did not rise.

I heard the faint distant sound of my brother and sisters calling out my name as my vision fade and I began to notice that my spirit is detached from my flesh. Behold, I began to see the light. As I approached and reached out toward it, I soon began to recognize the faces of my mother and father crying and calling family members.

I was hospitalized, and I just knew that this was my final hurrah. This is the moment I felt the sting of life. I didn't live out my purpose yet. I know I have more to live for than to die from a hornet attack.

I must survive, I must live, I can live, I will live, I rise.

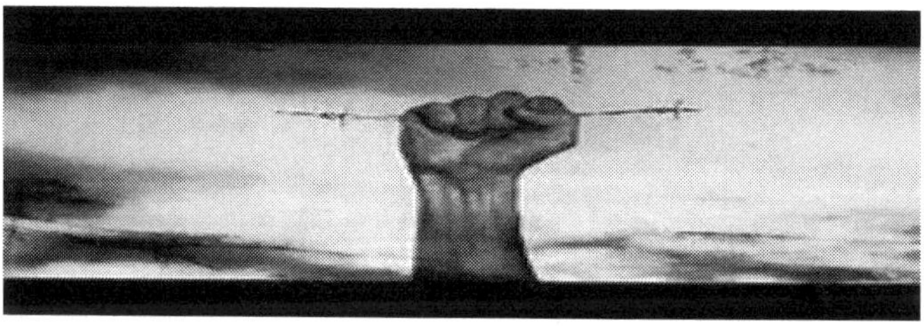

CHAPTER 4

What gives me the right?

"Every right has its responsibilities. Like the right itself, these responsibilities stem from no man-made law, but from the very nature of man and society. The security, progress, and welfare of one group is measured finally in the security, progress, and welfare of all mankind." Lewis Schwellenbach

My experiences and failures in life, the teaching of others and ultimately, the one who commanded me to get up and walk was my Father (God), he who have given me the instructions to lead his people out of the mindset of wobbling in their failures and use their failures for leverage for their successes.

This is my story; I was what you would call a "have not" coming up in East Saint Louis IL. One of the most uneducated, deficient and poverty locations in the United States of America. I don't agree with the statistic because it is my home. I must succeed to help home come up and out of the shadows of its past. Yes, my home, I love this place seeing that there are so much talent and quality here in ESTL.

There is a complete list of people that came up in the city of East Saint Louis and became very successful. Ike and Tina, Miles Davis, Jackie Joyner Kersey who is doing a lot for her city, Darius Miles, just to name a few. However, there are so many more successful people that came up and out.

Why is it that when we are exposed to a fantastic opportunity, we try to find all the negatives in it and never look at the great qualities that it will bring into our lives? However, when there is something very positive that comes up, we throw out the possible positives that were planned to be gained and accept the negative as our own. This is not surprising to me since it is what I have seen most of my life.

It is very baffling to me that this is supposed to be embraced by our children in our community or you become a sell out to your community. Not so, this is a mindset that needs to be broken. We must look at our circumstances differently and then you will find the good in it. Here is a poem that I would like you to read from top to bottom. Then read it from bottom to top.

"Today was the worst day ever
And don't try to convince me that
There's something good in every day
Because, when you take a closer look,
This world is a pretty evil place.
Even if
Some goodness does shine though once in a while
Satisfaction and happiness don't last.
And it's not true that
It's all in the mind and heart
Because
True happiness can be obtained
Only if one's surroundings are good
It's not true that good exists
I'm sure you can agree that
The reality
Creates
My attitude
It's all beyond my control
And you'll never in a million years hear me say that
Today was a good day."

Written by: NYC teen named Chanie Gorkins

We find ourselves so consumed with the issue that we consider ourselves in and never take the time to look at it in a positive way.

CHAPTER 5

The great division

"Divorce for child shakes trust in dependency on parents who now behave in an extremely undependable way. They surgically divide the family unit into two different households between which the child must learn to transit back and forth, for a while creating unfamiliarity, instability, and insecurity, never being able to be with one parent without having to be apart from the other."

Carl Pickhardt

Every child desire to have a mother and father under the same roof. Yes, my parents separated, and my world crumbled at that very moment it occurred. Homeless we became. We, a family of 6, my mother, two sisters, two brothers and I, moved in with my grandmother. She also had my two uncles, my aunt and her three children living there as well. That was a lot of people under one roof. The stress was high.

I remember the first week we were there. I was trying to get ice out of the ice tray and broke it. I told my mom and I received a different response from what I was expecting. I did some terrible things prior to this and I felt loved during my correction. But this time, I felt my mother's pain lash out on me. At that very point, I realized that my life will be different.

So, I knew to be careful of what I confess to my mom. My mom cried every night. She lost everything she worked so hard for, her world crumbled. I knew that my mom was strong. Seeing her break did something to me. I was only 7 years old. Nevertheless, I had to do something.

I began to think on what I can possibly do to change our circumstances and to be sure that she was comfortable and that she knew that we loved her through it all. Everything I did for her I tried to make it look like it was for a Queen. Because that's what she was in my eyes. I couldn't stand to see my mom struggle in that way.

During the midst of struggles, you will find strength. Pain is necessary, without it, one will never realize the injury, brokenness, nor the toxic portrayal you may be exposed to.

My parents fought from time to time physically as well as used and dealt drugs; however, financially strained. I've seen this at an early age and before the separation, I thought everything was normal and that was just how life is. It was painful, but we made it and now I can truly say that I learned from it.

I can remember not seeing my dad for months and I just knew he had forgotten about us. I was so confused because I knew my dad loved us and would do anything for us. But, I was giving up on him. Then came that day he arrived, his hands met and sandwiched my mother's hand so discretely to not be seen by her new man. I recalled that I've seen this transaction before but didn't articulate what was taking place. However, I did recall my mom taking us to purchase clothes shortly after.

I then began to understand that my dad was keeping the peace by sliding my mom money to take care of us and not causing friction with my mom's newly found male friend. I was slightly relieved that he was still supporting us. From that point, I knew my father was still there. My dad was willing to help us in whatever way he could, no matter what. But there was still a void in my heart that I couldn't shake. Because he was not there to talk to me when I needed him.

As I sat in a corner nearby the kitchen smelling the aroma of fried chicken cooking by the hands of my mom. I continued to play with my hot wheel cars and my GI Joes. Suddenly, there came a flow of tears pouring down my face, most would say were tears for no cause or reason. However, I knew exactly why I burst with tears out the blue.

I was aware of my family's situations and knew that times was only getting harder. I understood that my life will no longer be the same. My mom was heartbroken, my sisters were now dating. My oldest sister, the one who helped raise us moved out with her husband and my other older sister became the meanest person alive, at least that's what I thought. She was just trying to step up and make sure I become the man I was destined to be. She showed me how to respect females and what a woman desires a man to be. My big brother is now wilding and thuggish. My brother felt the same way about me as I felt about my younger brother. He struggled with being misplaced by our father and being the middle child was tough for him. He was the first son so I'm sure he had it harder. He showed me how to protect myself and how to reverse anything that most couldn't get out of. I used that throughout my entire life and we inherited another older brother and older sister from my mom male friend shortly after we moved. My younger brother was going through this with me, but we were too young to express neither our emotions to each other nor our siblings.

I remember the time where our electric was off for what seemed like months. Once our power was restored, we struggled even more than before. The food supply was short. We ate wish sandwiches, that is bread and mayo and wished we had meat in between. We ate crackers and butter as well as drank sugar water. Government peanut butter was the only thing that made us smile. It made the best peanut butter cookies ever.

I remember during the time our power was out, we ate boiled chicken and rice the entire month. I watched the neighbours across the alley beat a man with a 2×4 almost to death. Well, I'm not sure if he lived, I was young.

It was my first time seeing people cook rats, well that's what my brother told me. I was also too young to know for sure, but it smelled like it and we did have extremely large rats where we lived. I remember my stepfather shooting one in our front room. I believe it was already sick because it was moving very slowly. I thought it was a mole, nope, it was a rat.

So, anyway back to me and my moment of breakdown and the age of 8ish. I cried and cried until I decided to get up and do something. I got with my younger brother and my cousin. We sat down and came up with a plan on how we were going to get rich and help our parents.

We found out that we can earn money by collecting cans. But we couldn't possibly raise enough money fast enough to help our parents. So, we planned to raise money to get a game. The Sega Genesis was coming out and my mom was happy that we were trying to help ourselves, which would help them. So, she told us that she will match whatever we raised.

We were amazed, and we began to collect and collect and noticed that people were walking away with more money with smaller bags. What is going on, we asked? We came to find out they were putting rocks in the cans to make them heavier. Word? So, we decided that we should do the same. So off we go, putting rocks in the cans.

I promise we couldn't get away with nothing. Immediately, they checked our bags and outcome the rocks. We raised enough for our game, but we learned a more valuable lesson that day. That day made our lives from that point forward. It taught us that we will be held at a higher standard than our surrounding peers and elders.

I also experienced a classmate during elementary school handle a situation that changed my life. It was during class one day and the teacher and this young lady were called into the hall and it seemed like they were out there forever. She walked back into the class with the teacher alongside her sobbing. However, this young lady walked in, grabbed her things and proceeded to leave. She lost her mother and I couldn't understand at that age how that could happen especially to her. She was always the mature and respectful student in the class. She stayed two blocks passed my house and I watched her walk home daily from school to make sure she doesn't break down. But, she walked with her head held up and continued to do well in class. So, every year on her birthday, I made sure I called her to wish her a happy birthday as a remembrance of saving a life during the loss of one. Thank you, M.S.

We are required to do things with integrity. Anytime we tried to take the low road we got caught. So, we decided to just work hard and have compassion for the ones we encounter and for the things we desire no matter what people are doing around us. This experience helped us stay away from doing and selling illegal substance, robbing, stealing and many other characters diminishing decisions once we got older.

CHAPTER

6

How did I become motivated?

*"Passion is the Fuel to Success, Yield but don't Stop,
Cry but keep Pressing, have pain but don't die."*

I was sitting in my room one day as a teen thinking and thought of everything that I did that was not productive in my life. It was so funny to me the things that I did with my time, and then it began to be sad. I was always planning to become a very successful person in life, but I never followed through with the things I planned to do to accomplish my goals. Instead, I began to try to do things that will pull me from the task that will bring me closer to my goals.

I liked playing video games, sleeping, and flirting with the ladies. What silly things I did to pass time. I called one of the girl's numbers and her mother answered. "May I speak to Jazz." I said with a very respectful tone. "What do you want with Jazz young man, she is getting ready for church; do you want to go?" She responded. I denied being able to go for months but she never gave in. Every time I called, she asked but for some reason, I kept calling; then one day I said yes, I am dressed and ready.

I began to go to church and found that there are different people in the world and not just on television with athletes, actors, and musicians. There were strong, powerful, and wealthy men in the church running very successful businesses. I thought that you were supposed to not have a financial gain in this world as a Christian.

I was wowed at all of this, for I was never exposed to this kind of lifestyle growing up in East Saint Louis; until my mid-teens. Now, this was amazing, these men were tangible and one thing I did know was how to approach someone with respect.

I longed to connect with successful men that were getting it legally.

I was so used to seeing financial success from the street pharmacist if you know what I mean.

Growing up in my house with my dad and mom required the upmost respect out of us. Yes, sir and ma'am every time we responded to them, absolutely no lying or else, and do as we say and not as we do go deep in our family. My parents were always in survival mode trying to take care of all five of us. This paid off as I began to step out as a young man into the journey that God has given me.

I was introduced to mentorship by my Bishop. Bishop Tolar is his name and he began to guide me in a direction that developed me in a way I always dreamed of, what an amazing tool to success.

My mentor helped and guided me through the trials and obstacles of life. He showed me how to go in and out before people and when to speak and when not to speak. He always said to me in order to be a great leader, you must first be a great follower of a great leader and to be a great teacher, you must first be a great listener of a great teacher.

These tools took me a long way in my journey to success. I began to offer to do tasks in exchange for wisdom. I kept a notepad always, I never knew when I will be introduced to a teachable moment.

Now, the craziest thing happened to me one day I was with my mentor, I did something incorrectly and I was corrected at that point, and I learned a valuable lesson. I learned that being corrected is more valuable than getting everything right while being mentored. Why? You may say; if you get everything correct, are you learning anything new and/are you removing any unhealthy habits? Being corrected, you will begin to increase as a person and only then you can become successful in life.

CHAPTER

7

How bad do you want it?

"When you want to succeed as bad as you want to breathe, then you'll become successful" (Eric Thomas)

My God, I am so hungry for successful change, aren't you? I am so tired of the struggle; I have struggled all my life. If my breath was connected to my success I would have suffocated. Thank God it wasn't. However, I am so hungry for success that I want it as bad as I want to breathe.

Yes, I am so excited that you are on this journey with me because it is about time for us to make some positive changes in our lives. It has been far too long living in the slums of life. How in the world are we going to do anything for ourselves and our families if we don't get up and do what God called us to do for ourselves and our families?

We have so many people connected to us and our success. We can't afford to dwell in our failures. Failing does not make you a failure but develops an expert in the area that you failed in. We can't complete our purpose without discomfort.

I have never experienced a bodybuilder gain muscle without first destroying the muscle first. The muscle begins to build and respond to the prior tare of the muscles and develop much stronger and bigger muscles.

We must believe in ourselves before others will believe. That means we cannot wait for approval from others when you are setting a trend to follow. You are the lead and will go down that journey alone. You are the only one that knows what God has given and tasked you to do. Don't talk about it, be about it.

I'm not telling you to be better than another person. I'm telling you to be better than you are right now. You must continue to strive to be the best that you can be. Be the most perfect self you can be, be the expert of who you are and know who you are and grow from there. You will find that the moment you learn who you are is the very moment you will become valuable in the lives of the ones you love and the ones that are watching you from a distant. That's all to it.

Work on you and only you. It's contagious, people see one being great and it inspires them to strive to be great. Children live out an unsuccessful or successful life because of the inspiration of the ones before them. So, if you are not inspired, surround yourself around inspired people.

Let me share with you a short story about the behavior of the carrots, eggs and coffee beans.

"A young woman went to her mother and told her about her life and how things were so hard for her. She did not know how she was going to make it and wanted to give up. She was tired of fighting and struggling. It seemed as one problem was solved, a new one arose.

Her mother took her to the kitchen. She filled three pots with water and placed each on a high fire. Soon the pots came to boil. In the first, she placed carrots, in the second she placed eggs, and in the last, she placed ground coffee beans. She let them sit and boil without saying a word.

In about twenty minutes, she turned off the burners. She fished the carrots out and placed them in a bowl. She pulled the eggs out and placed them in a bowl. Then she ladled the coffee out and placed it in a bowl. Turning to her daughter, she asked, "Tell me, what do you see?" Carrots, eggs, and coffee," she replied.

Her mother brought her closer and asked her to feel the carrots. She did and noted that they were soft. The mother then asked the daughter to take an egg and break it. After pulling off the shell, she observed the hard-boiled egg. Finally, the mother asked the daughter to sip the coffee. The daughter smiled as she tasted its rich aroma. The daughter then asked, "What does it mean, mother?"

Her mother explained that each of these objects had faced the same adversity – boiling water. Each reacted differently. The carrot went in strong, hard, and unrelenting. However, after being subjected to the boiling water, it softened and became weak. The egg had been fragile. Its thin outer shell had protected its liquid interior, but after sitting through the boiling water, its inside became hardened. The coffee beans were unique, however. After they were in the water, they had changed the water.

"Which are you?" she asked her daughter. When adversity knocks on your door, how do you respond? Are you a carrot, an egg or coffee bean?"

Are you the carrot that seems strong, but with pain and adversity wilts, becomes soft and loses its strength? Are you the egg that starts with a malleable heart, but changes with the heat? Does your shell look the same, but on the inside are you bitter and tough with a stiff spirit and hardened heart?

Or are you the coffee bean? Changing the hot water, the very circumstance that brings the pain. When the water gets hot, it releases the fragrance and flavor. If you are like the bean, when things are at their worst, you get better and change the situation around you. When the hour is the darkest and trials are their greatest, do you elevate yourself to another level?"

Are you a carrot, an egg, or a coffee bean? How have you reacted to adversity? We must understand that we will have pain with anything worth striving for. How bad do you want it, soldier? How bad do you want it?

CHAPTER
8

F.O.C.U.S

FREEDOM FROM FEAR WILL ALLOW YOU TO OVERCOME OBSTACLES WITH CONFIDENCE FOR UNLIMITED SUCCESS

We cannot continue to walk this life as if we have no purpose or clue to what we should be doing with our lives. We are never too old to learn and never too young to teach. We have only one job to do and that is the work of the Lord. We are ambassadors of Christ and we are placed here for a purpose, never allow anyone to take you off that journey for your journey is your path to the Promised Land.

Fear has taken over our mindsets for as long as I can remember. Let's break the link of fear and connect to the Freedom train. Freedom is a mindset we must train the mind to respond to; this freedom includes opportunities that will deliver us from Fear.

The Lord is my shepherd;
I shall not want.
2 He makes me to lie down in green pastures;
He leads me beside the still waters.
3 He restores my soul;
He leads me in the paths of righteousness
For His name's sake.

4 Yea, though I walk through the valley of the shadow of death,
I will fear no evil;
For You are with me;
Your rod and Your staff, they comfort me.

5 You prepare a table before me in the presence of my enemies;
You anoint my head with oil;
My cup runs over.
6 Surely goodness and mercy shall follow me

All the days of my life;
And I will dwell[a] in the house of the Lord
Forever.

The Bible - Psalm 23: 1-6

Whenever I am afraid, I will trust in You. In God (I will praise His word), In God I have put my trust; I will not fear. What can flesh do to me?

The Bible - Psalm 56:3-4

Obstacles have been placed in our lives only to make us stronger and more prepared for the race of life. We must overcome them to be able to compete in the finals of life. Overcome by taking on the obstacles head-on, you must embrace the challenges, stand your ground, endure to the end, and stay on your feet. If you do fall, fall on your back, because if you can look up, you can get up.

You will keep him in perfect peace, whose mind is stayed on You, because he trusts in You.

The Bible - Isaiah 26:3,

Do not be overcome by evil but overcome evil with good.

The Bible - Romans 12:21

So many of us walk around with a false reality of Confidence! The standard is set way too low and the reality is that you all succeed at reaching that level of success. However, it is set on an all-time low according to the surrounding areas. Set a higher standard for yourself and if you come short of it, you will succeed in preparation for the real challenge (the world): what is Confidence and how should it be presented? Confidence is the ability to strive for something that has not ever been obtained by you and others around you.

I can do all things through Christ[a] who strengthens me.

The Bible - Philippians 4:13,

Therefore, do not cast away your confidence, which has great reward. For you have need of endurance, so that after you have done the will of God, you may receive the promise:

The Bible - Hebrews 10:35-36

Wow, unlimited sound amazing but so many times we find that unlimited failure is all around us daily. It's so hard to see success in our daily lives. Stop for a moment and just look at the situations and I am sure you will find that you can have Success in more areas of your life than you thought. Unlimited Success is available to you, if only you will believe. Put in hard direct work toward your goals and you will see Unlimited Success. Just look at one Success at a time.

Delight yourself also in the Lord, and He shall give you the desires of your heart.

The Bible - Psalm 37:4,

Humble yourselves in the sight of the Lord, and He will lift you up.

The Bible - James 4:10,

Commit your works to the Lord, and your thoughts will be established.

The Bible - Proverbs 16:3

I refuse to lay down in the failures of life beaten down and hang ups. I am powerful and strong. Hercules does not have anything on me for he was born strong with no life experiences. I am the overcomer, the one who has slapped defeat dead in the mouth and walked forward with my head held high.

My life hard comings have made me strong and I'm victorious at all the battles come up against me. The Dominion is mine and weakness is not an option, but power, love, and a sound mind. Watch me fly, fly to the highest heights. Glory to God that I did not die but I have risen above my night and the brighter day has come to sight. Praise to God the glorious Light of my life.

We as young adults must live a life that is very difficult but not impossible. The Impossible is possible for that is what we call Faith, and my bishop has instilled this in me often. So, I ask that you say this with me with power and conviction.

THE REST OF MY LIFE WILL BE

THE BEST OF MY LIFE (Repeat 3x)

CHAPTER 9

Testimony

Plant a seed, eventually, it will grow. It may not grow in your season, but it will grow in the seasons to come. So plant good seeds for the sake of your children and your children's children.

Why do we hide our problems as if we can solve them ourselves? God knows our struggles and our outcomes. I've hidden from God a few times myself, believe it or not. I'm almost sure you did too.

During a time in my life, I thought that my life had neither value nor meaning and began to live a life that led me to a dead-end. There were things that happened in my life that I felt was a curse. I recognized it when I was a teen.

I started a record label with my cousins and shortly after, I began to be recognized by everyone in the industry.

This could have been the best part of waking up; people flocking to you for leadership. The haters have no love for a brother only means to destroy.

So, as time went by, I found myself in the club every night drinking and partying, getting back home around 6 to 7 AM not knowing how I made it into my driveway. I was a mess;

I began to lose family members left and right including my mom. My cousin was murdered; he was shot in the neck; my uncle was robbed and killed, shot in both knees and bled to death, my cousin was being chased and crashed and burned to death, my uncle was murdered and was stabbed in the neck, my stepfather overdosed or died from carbon dioxide poisoning, my mom passed away from pneumonia and I had a head-on collision which landed me on bed rest for over a month.

Shortly after these occurrences, I had two car thefts, house broken into, and I began to chase and ram cars, kick in doors, plot to put people in trunks and blow up houses. I was homeless, and I began to sell drugs. Now all of this occurred in less than two years. This was my breaking point to decide.

As I sat on this soggy half burned bed and begin to look around. I noticed every memory that I had of my mom burned to crisp. I began to stare at the moon through the burnt roof and began to think of ways to remove the pain. I began to look down the barrel of this 8-shooter revolver, assured that it was locked and loaded.

I pressed the gun to the temple of my head and thought about the pros and cons of what my actions will cause. How will my family continue? Will they blame themselves for me taking my own life? Will I be selfish for ending my life and leaving my loved ones with unanswered questions? However, I just wanted to remove the pain, it was too unbearable.

Suddenly, a voice came to me in the sound of my Bishop saying, son do you know what your purpose is for your life? This is what was always asked of me when I went to church to repent. God has been speaking all along knowing that this time will come. These very few words saved my life.

We do have haters out their trying to stop this from happening, but we have overcome them so far and continue to be victorious in all the obstacles that challenge us.

Love harder than your enemies hate and then you shall be victorious over the challenges of the enemy

THE Struggle IS REAL

CHAPTER 10

The Numb Experience

"Emotional numbness is a defense mechanism employed by the mind to avoid intense and overwhelming emotions such as fear, hatred, jealousy, and grief." Aletheia Luna

"I can't take this no more, it hurts to bad and it's stinging and burning. WHY, why did this happen to me? I didn't do anything wrong, I was just trying to help, I am so tired of people, this life and the things I must go through to live in this world are driving me into an early grave. I am tired, so tired of this life. I just can't take this anymore.

Every time I take one step toward greatness, it seems to take me into more pain and discomfort. Why do I have to go through so much to become great? I hate you, Yes, I hate you, and I can't do this anymore." While I glazed deeply at myself in the mirror saying these heart wrenching words. I began to feel this warm tingling feeling inside of me.

It felt as if a clean sweep came over me because my thoughts instantly began to be encouraging thoughts that have been put within me over the years from books, mentors and great people that have encouraged me from my past. The words go a little like this; you are more than a conquer, and you're great beyond measure, you have the power to accomplish all that you can imagine or think.

> ***Let us not become weary in doing good, for the proper time we will reap a harvest if we do not give up. Galatians 6:9***
>
> ***Perseverance must finish its work so that you may be mature and complete, not lacking anything. James 1:4-5***

You must take control of your imagination. When I was homeless I could have given up, when I was standing and watching my mother take her last breath, I could have given up, when I lost my grandmother, my two uncles, my three cousins, my job, my house, my cars, my mind and very close to taking my life in a matter of a years' time, I could have just thrown in the towel and given up. But God had a purpose for me.

Through all that heartache and pain, I did not give in. It was necessary for me to feel the pain of loss, hurt, and abandonment. I felt helpless and hopeless my life was over, as far as I was concerned. I had to press through the process more than ever before. My life had to change. I had to take a turn for a purpose.

So, if I left this earth today, I will feel no remorse for the loved ones that I have left behind. Because I know I have given them my all. My all is the purpose I was here on this earth. I must be a good steward over this life I was given. It is a dangerous feeling to know that you are in a position where you can't do anything to change your situation.

I have learned that in every situation you encounter, you can make something out of it that will become something good. Now, pain can put you in a situation where you will either become numb to it or it will put you in a position where you can place it under your feet.

So that every time you become stagnant in your purpose, the heat of pain will place you on so much heat you will begin to press to get so far from it, that it will force you into success and purpose. Use your pain for the encouragement to continue, not quit; for that pain is underneath you, not on top of you. Climb higher and higher to your destiny.

ABOUT THE AUTHOR

Well if you read this in its entirety you learned about my childhood. I'm a husband, father of three, and father/mentor to 100s more. I still serve in the city of East Saint Louis IL as well as any other city that sees value in my presence. I love speaking to youths and young adults about pursuing greatness.

I also don't mind being transparent to reach a child dark place if that is what is needed to bring them out into their destiny. Well, that's who I am and will share more of my juicy teen and young adult years in my next vol. of Life stings. Love you to success.

Be blessed,

You can leave a book review or go sign up on my email list for a special bonus or follow me on

Facebook: www.facebook.com/LifeStings

Instagram/Twitter: @Lifestings

Email: Lifestings@gmail.com

Website: www.Kingdomempowered.org/Lifestings

ACKNOWLEDGMENTS

I will first like to give praises to my father, God, and Lord Jesus Christ. Ok, my friends, family, and supporters. You all have been some of the most supportive people I have ever seen. Thank you all so much for encouraging me to overcome my greatest fear. Yes cousin's, I will be talking about our episodes in volume II, Love ya. Bishop, thank you for being led by the Holy Spirit and in truth when it came to me pursuing what God had for me to do. You a true man of God. To my three lovely children, Larry, Jehireh, and Jehda, you all give me life. When I cried out to God for a family, he gave me his best. I love you three blessings with all my heart. To you my wife, my Queen, the next page is for you babe.

To my love. You are my Queen, the only one for me. The one that causes my jaws to drop when my eyes met God's perfect idea of a woman. That's you, my LOVE. I lay my head in your bosom and find peace, a sense of belonging. You are the pinnacle of my tower of success and fuel to my drive. You are my mother's Sunday dinner to my hunger for living life. You are the assigned spirit to my soul. I love you my Queen, my Rib, the mother of my children, my wife. Never lose sight of that.

Signed
Your King

THE OVERCOMER CREED

I refuse to lay down in the failures of life beaten down and hang ups. I am powerful and strong. Hercules does not have anything on me for he was born strong with no life experiences. I am the overcomer the one who has slapped defeat dead in the mouth and walked forward with my head held high. My life hard comings have made me strong and I'm victorious at all the battles that come up against me. The Dominion is mine and weakness is not an option, but power, love, and a sound mind. Watch me fly, fly to the highest heights. Glory to God that I did not die but I have risen above my night and the brighter day has come to sight.

Praise to God the glorious Light of my life.

We as young adults must live a life that is very difficult but not impossible. The Impossible is possible for that is what we call Faith, and our Bishops have instilled this in us often. So, I ask that you say this with me with power and conviction.

THE REST OF MY LIFE WILL BE

THE BEST OF MY LIFE (Repeat x3)

Thanks for reading! Please add a brief review

on Amazon and let me know your thought!

18554828R00039

Made in the USA
Lexington, KY
27 November 2018